FEEL THE FORCE

Ride That ROLLER COASTER!

Forces at an Amusement Park

Richard and Louise Spilsbury

heinemann
raintree

To contact Capstone Global Library please call 800-747-4992, or visit our web site www.capstonepub.com

Edited by Helen Cox Cannons and Holly Beaumont
Designed by Philippa Jenkins
Original illustrations © Capstone Global Libary Ltd 2015
Illustrated by HL Studios, Witney, Oxon, England
Picture research by Tracy Cummins
Production by Helen McCreath
Originated by Capstone Global Library Ltd
Printed and Bound in China by Leo Paper Group

19 18 17 16 15
10 9 8 7 6 5 4 3 2 1

Library of Congress Cataloging-in-Publication Data
Cataloging-in-publication data is available at the Library of Congress.
ISBN 978-1-4846-2598-9 (hardback)
ISBN 978-1-4846-2603-0 (paperback)
ISBN 978-1-4846-2613-9 (ebook PDF)

Acknowledgments
We would like to thank the following for permission to reproduce photographs: Alamy Images: Gaertner, 31, imageBROKER, 14, Kim Karpeles, 37, Stockshoot, 40; AP Photo: HO, 19, Wong Maye-E, 39; Capstone Press: HL Studios, 7, 15, 23, 27, Karon Dubke, 10, 11, 24, 25, 32, 33; Corbis: Macduff Everton, 12, 42 Middle, REUTERS/Dave Kaup, 13; Dreamstime: Gow927, 29; Getty Images: ATABOY, 6, 43 Bottom, Johannes Simon, 17, Zia Soleil, 36; Rex USA: Mikael Buck/Rex, 38; Courtesy of Simworx Limited: www.siwmorx.co.uk, 34; Shutterstock: 2009fotofriends, 8, 42 Top, jabiru, Front Cover, Racheal Grazias, 4, 21, Ruslan Kerimov, 18, Ta Khum, 9; SuperStock: imageBROKER, 30; Thinkstock: Jupiterimages, Design Element, 42 Bottom, Marcio Silva, 26, 43 Top, Design Element, Purestock, 5; Wikimedia: flickr/themeparkgc, 41.

We would like to thank Patrick O'Mahony for his invaluable help in the preparation of this book.

Every effort has been made to contact copyright holders of material reproduced in this book. Any omissions will be rectified in subsequent printings if notice is given to the publisher.

Contents

Some words are shown in bold, **like this**. You can find out what they mean by looking in the glossary.

What Draws People to the Park?

Where can you plummet to the ground, hang upside down, spin around, bump, and get splashed, all in one day? No, not in a waterfall or an enormous washing machine, but at an amusement park! Millions of people visit amusement parks each year to experience a variety of thrills all in one place. Never mind the lines—some of these could be the rides of your life.

Motion and forces

The one thing all the rides at an amusement park have in common is motion. Things only move with a push or pull. Without these **forces**, objects stay still, or they continue moving just as they were. All forces result from the interactions between two objects. Most forces involve contact— you kick a stationary soccer ball and it rolls or flies away.

With so many rides, there are many chances to feel the power of forces and their effects.

Experiencing the forces of the amusement park feels dangerous, but it is safe fun.

Forces work in pairs. When the forces acting on an object are equal, or **balanced**, then the object stays in the same place or moves at a constant speed. To make an object start moving, or to change its speed or direction, we have to make one force larger than another so they are **unbalanced**. Half of the fun of the rides at an amusement park is the way they speed us up and slow us down, lift us high and drop us suddenly. So, exactly what forces are at work?

SPEED AND ACCELERATION

Speed is a measure of how fast something is going. Push off on a skateboard and it would keep going at that speed forever—if there weren't other forces to slow it down. These include the force caused by its wheels rubbing against the ground, called **friction**. But if you kept pushing while the skateboard was moving, it would get faster. The rate of change of speed is called **acceleration**.

Can you feel the force?

The most important of all the forces in action at an amusement park is also the one that keeps us on Earth: **gravity**. Wherever you are and whatever you're doing on Earth, gravity is pulling you toward the ground. Gravity is a **noncontact force**. We cannot feel it directly, but we do feel it indirectly. Sit on a chair and you can feel the upward push of the material the chair is made from, resulting from the downward pull on your body. That's what we feel as weight.

On a downward roller coaster ride, you feel the pull of gravity toward Earth as the push of the safety bar into your stomach or chest.

TERMINAL VELOCITY

When skydivers jump from a plane, they speed up as they fall. They reach a top speed of around 150 miles (240 kilometers) per hour just 12 seconds after jumping. We call this speed **terminal velocity**. They reach terminal velocity when their weight is balanced by air resistance.

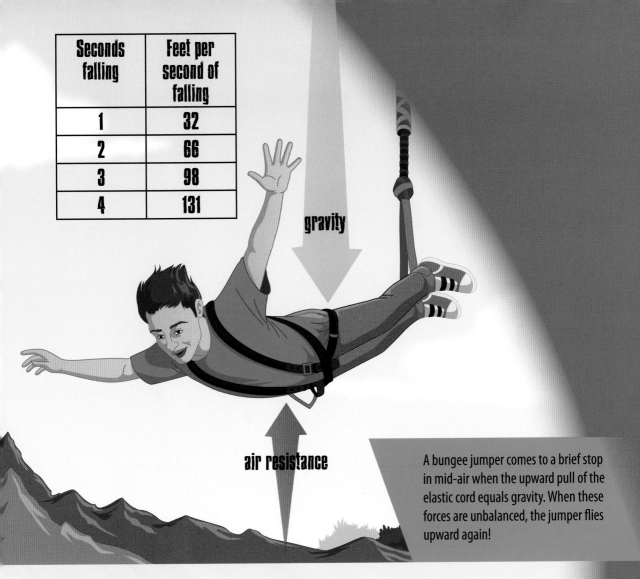

Seconds falling	Feet per second of falling
1	32
2	66
3	98
4	131

gravity

air resistance

A bungee jumper comes to a brief stop in mid-air when the upward pull of the elastic cord equals gravity. When these forces are unbalanced, the jumper flies upward again!

Falling objects

We can use gravity to move. When you drop from the top point of a roller coaster, gravity pulls you and the seat you are in downward. The force of gravity also causes things to speed up as they fall, which is what helps make rides so exciting—and scary! This is because the force of gravity causes acceleration when a moving object goes downhill.

The reason things don't just keep falling faster and faster when they are dropping downward is that the opposing forces act to slow them down. These include the upward push of air, or **air resistance**. A roller coaster track also has brakes to slow down its movement for safety, but you will still feel the fear!

Why Do I Feel Lighter as I Fall?

Screams ring in your ears as you fall, and you feel strangely light as the ground hurtles toward you. These are the unforgettable sensations of a trip on a free-fall ride or drop tower. On a free-fall ride:

- Passengers are safely strapped in seats in a car.
- Powerful motors pull the car up a **vertical** track up to 415 feet (126 meters) above the ground.
- The car stops, leaving passengers hanging in mid-air.
- Brakes are released and the car falls.

At zero g, people feel lighter, even though they are the same **mass**. This is because there is less upward force acting to slow them down than if they were on the ground.

VOMIT COMET!

Astronauts experience zero g (zero gravity) in space because the pull of gravity from Earth is much weaker. They train for spending time in space in special airplanes that fly very high and then dive downward. Inside the airplane, people can float around and experience weightlessness for several minutes in zero-g conditions before the plane has to level out. People who are not used to the feeling often feel sick and even vomit (throw up). That's how the plane got its name!

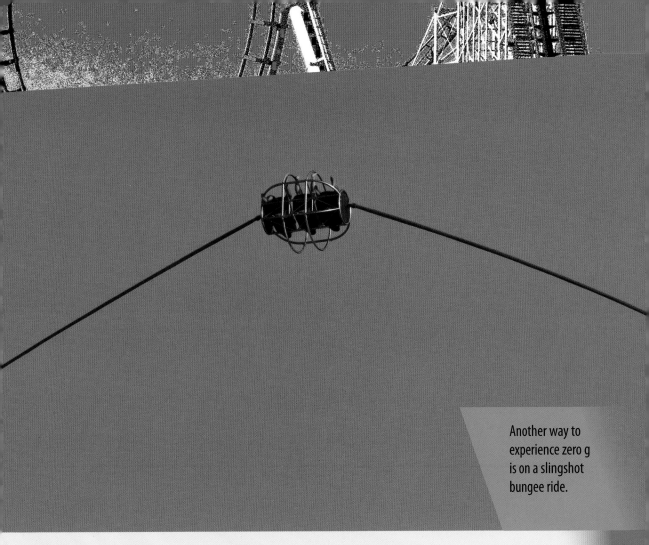

G-force

G-force is a way to describe the forces acting on someone in comparison to gravity. In the first few seconds of falling, people in a car or compartment feel as if their seats are dropping away. They experience **weightlessness** because they and their seats are accelerating at the same rate. They feel no upward push from the seat and experience **zero g**, even though gravity is still pulling them to Earth.

Slowing down

Cars don't crash into the ground on a free-fall ride because tracks gradually curve toward the ground. The upward push from the track slows the car's acceleration. Then, it reaches a horizontal stretch of track and the brakes go on to **decelerate** the car until it reaches a standstill.

ACTIVITY: Weightless Water

Try this simple demonstration of zero g using a cup of water. It is best to do it with two people and in a place where it is okay to spill water, such as outside or over a large bucket.

You will need:
- plastic or paper cups
- hole punch or sharp pencil
- jug of water
- video camera
- sturdy chair

1 Make a hole about ¼ in. (½ cm) in diameter halfway down the cup using the hole punch or pencil. (Sharp pencils can also pierce skin, so ask an adult for help to avoid any injuries.)

2 One person operates the video camera and the other holds the cup.

3 Cover the hole with a finger, fill the cup with water, and record what happens when you uncover the hole.

4 Climb CAREFULLY on the chair and repeat step 3, but drop the cup as you uncover the hole.

5 The fall only lasts a few seconds, so you may have to repeat until you get some good film of what happens. Repeat step 1 if your cup breaks when hitting the ground.

Conclusion

It is easier to see what happens if you watch the recordings in slow motion. Gravity pulls on water in the cup, but it only spills out when the hole is uncovered. This is because there is no balancing force pushing back on the water. Once the water level is below the hole, it stops pouring out. Water does not come out of the open hole while the cup falls. This is because the water is accelerating as fast as the cup, and the downward force of gravity is balanced by the upward push from the cup. The water shoots out once the cup hits the ground because it topples over.

How Do I Slide So Fast?

For gentler sliding fun, you can take a ride on a playground slide. But for maximum speed—and a soaking—always choose the waterslide.

Working against gravity

A slide is a slope that applies a force working against gravity. On a shallow slide, the downward pull of gravity is only just bigger than the upward push from the slide, so you slip down slowly. On a steep slide, there is very little upward push from the slide, so you slide down quickly. All waterslides have sides so that you don't slip off the edges as you move along them.

SLOWING DOWN WITH FRICTION

The brakes that control and stop many amusement park rides work by using friction. Powerful electric machines push pads against metal underneath the moving cars to increase contact. Designers may also use water to increase friction. After a steep waterslide, riders sometimes enter a water-filled canal to slow them down.

Riders of this waterslide enter a clear pipe, through which they see sharks in the water!

On some enormous waterslides, passengers shoot down in rafts for added protection from any bumps.

Making contact

A book slides faster across a polished hardwood floor than a carpet because of the contact force called friction. Friction acts in the opposite direction than motion. It is greater when sliding faster and when one or both of the surfaces are rough, since there is greater contact between them. Friction burns can happen on playground slides because motion energy is converted to heat energy due to friction. Imagine this happening on a steep slide dozens of feet long!

Reducing the rub

Slide designers reduce friction and increase speed at amusement parks in different ways. On some slides, people slide on smooth mats that protect them from any friction burns. Waterslides have a constant flow of water trickling down the slide. This prevents friction by forming a slippery water layer between rider and slide.

Am I Going to Fly off This Ride?

Some amusement park rides put you in a spin. Scramblers and octopuses move very fast in circles, and riders feel like they are going to fly off the ride. There is one thing clearly to blame: **centripetal force**.

What is centripetal force?

Centripetal force is a force that comes into play when acceleration happens in a curve or a circle. It pushes moving objects inward toward the center of a curve. Imagine you are sitting on a spinning scrambler. As you spin in one direction, you are actually moving outward at right angles to the path of the curve at any point. You don't fly off because centripetal force pulls you inward along the arm of the scrambler.

It is difficult to escape the feeling of being thrown out of the car until the scrambler slows down and the centripetal force gets smaller.

USING CENTRIPETAL FORCE

Amusement parks are not the only places where centripetal force is in demand. It is often used to separate materials, because the force is greater on objects with greater density, or mass, for a given size. For example, centripetal force separates the water from the clothing in a spin dryer.

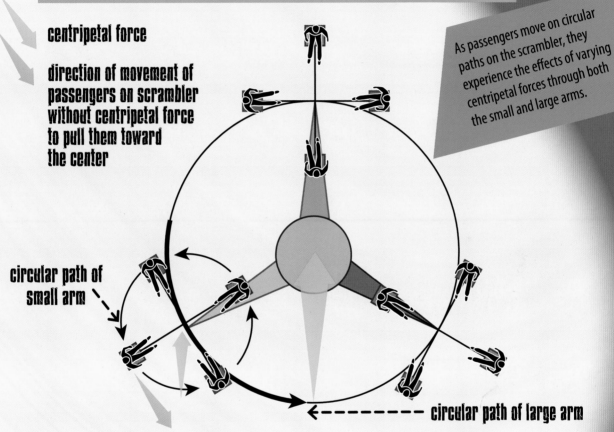

centripetal force

direction of movement of passengers on scrambler without centripetal force to pull them toward the center

As passengers move on circular paths on the scrambler, they experience the effects of varying centripetal forces through both the small and large arms.

circular path of small arm

circular path of large arm

The centripetal experience

You experience the centripetal force as a strong push in your side from the edge of the car as you travel around a bend. Centripetal force is greater when an object is moving faster and also when the distance from the center of rotation to the object is smaller. Ride designers make passengers feel changing centripetal force by having small rotating arms on larger rotating arms. They also increase the sense of danger by making passengers in one car spin very close to those in others.

Why is the ground opening up?

You start a kind of ride known as a rotor or gravitron by walking inside a circular room and standing against the wall. Once several riders are inside, the door shuts and it gradually spins faster and faster. After a while, the floor of the room opens up, yet you do not slip down the wall. You feel pinned there. What's going on?

Sticking to the wall

Riders stick to the wall because of centripetal force and friction. The ride spins at over 20 complete **revolutions** per minute. At this speed, there is strong centripetal force. This increases the contact of people's bodies against the wall so much that the forces are balanced. This means the riders won't fall or slide down the wall once the floor opens. Sliding down happens gradually once the ride slows down and gravity gets the upper hand!

Evolution of spinning rides

This kind of ride was invented in 1949, but it was not the first popular spinning amusement park ride. The joy wheel from the early 20th century, for example, was a conical, polished disc riders sat on that spun around faster and faster. It gradually threw all the riders off into the crowd because the ride had no walls!

WHAT IS CENTRIFUGAL FORCE?

The outward pull we feel on the rotor, scrambler, or any ride that happens in a circle is often called centrifugal force. But most scientists agree that this force does not exist. They say that you or any object can only move in a circle if there is an inward centripetal force stopping you from flying off in a straight line. What you feel is simply your body's interpretation of that inward push.

The rotor ride is a popular feature of German Oktoberfest celebrations. You can ride upright on the rotor, at an angle, or even upside down!

How Does a Roller Coaster Work?

Most people go to amusement parks for the roller coasters. What other ride gives you high speeds, zero-g straight falls, extreme turns and twists, hanging upside down, and other sensations, all in one package?

Building a ride

Vehicles called cars move along tracks supported by giant beams, columns, or other strong structures. The tracks and supports can be made largely of wood, but most are usually all steel. Cars have seats for riders that can be mounted on top or hang underneath. Some even spin around during the ride. The cars roll along the track on tough plastic wheels that produce low friction, which helps them to move fast. There are wheels on the top, side, and bottom of the track so that they grip the car to the track whichever way it is thrown during the ride.

Getting started

Once the riders are all safely buckled in, most roller coaster cars are pulled upward to the top of the first hill. Most roller coasters have a loop of tough chain that is moved around wheels turned by electric motors. The chain is continually moving up the hill. Metal hooks underneath each car attach to the chain to hitch a ride to the top. Some roller coasters have launch systems using magnets, the push of compressed air, or other forces to speed them up the hill.

Roller coaster cars have wheels above and below to make sure the train grips to the tracks, even when taking tight corners or hanging upside down.

MAGNET BLASTOFF

The fastest catapult-launch roller coasters can accelerate from 0 to 150 miles (0 to 240 kilometers) per hour in just five seconds. They have special electric motors to create powerful magnets underneath the car and on the track below. By changing the electricity flow, the magnets pull toward or push away from each other. The cars can speed along the tracks using these pushes and pulls.

Magnetic launchers use lots of electricity to create the powerful magnets needed to carry roller coaster cars up tracks.

acceleration from magnetic launchers

19

What happens during the first fall?

At the top of the first big hill, the roller coaster cars are standing alone. There is no more power from motors to move them along until the end of the ride. But how does a heavy roller coaster get the energy it needs to keep going?

Storing and using energy

You might not know it, but a roller coaster rising up a hill is busy storing energy. Energy is the ability to do work. The stored energy in the roller coaster is **potential energy**, which results from its height above the ground. It has more if it goes higher, because gravity will have a greater distance to use the energy to speed the roller coaster downhill. The potential energy then changes into movement, or **kinetic energy**. A roller coaster has its biggest store of this as it speeds into the foot of the first hill.

Rising again

Then, roller coaster cars often rise up another hill. This is when most of the kinetic energy starts to change back into potential energy. The upward movement is slowed not only by the downward pull of gravity, but also by the slight friction between the wheels and the track, and air resistance. But people design roller coasters so that the height of the first hill allows cars to store enough energy to not come to a halt until the end of the ride.

CONSERVATION OF ENERGY

Turn on a switch and electrical energy turns to light energy from a lamp. A car engine changes chemical energy in fuel into kinetic energy. Energy never disappears—it just changes form. We call this conservation of energy. In any machine, not all energy changes into the form that is needed. For example, laptop computers give off heat energy as they use electrical energy for computing tasks.

A roller coaster is an energy-converting scream machine!

decreasing potential energy

increasing kinetic energy

friction and air resistance

gravity

What Happens in a Loop-the-Loop?

Climb steeply, travel backward upside down, and then plummet downhill. This is what happens in a loop-the-loop. What is amazing about this roller coaster feature is that it packs a punch by changing forces in a trip lasting just a few seconds.

On a loop-the-loop, one second you're feeling heavier than ever, and the next as light as a feather. This is because of acceleration due to gravity and centripetal forces.

centripetal force

acceleration force

gravity

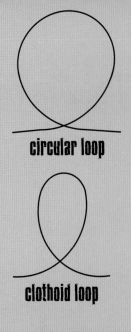

circular loop

clothoid loop

The g-force journey

On entering the loop, the car's acceleration force is pointing forward and gravity is pointing downward. The upward push from the seat makes you feel heavier than ever. You are experiencing high g-forces. In an instant, the car is pointing upward and gravity is pulling downward. Centripetal acceleration is making you feel as if you are being pushed against the side of the loop. Then you are hanging upside down and briefly experience near zero g because there is no upward force to push against gravity. The g-force then rises as the car zooms downward and reaches the end of the loop-the-loop.

The energy flip

The loop-the-loop is not only a place where forces change, but also where energy changes form from kinetic to potential in an instant. But it can only work if the roller coaster car accelerates fast and has enough kinetic energy to carry it upside down through the top of the loop. Without the right speeds, cars would slow and not complete the ride.

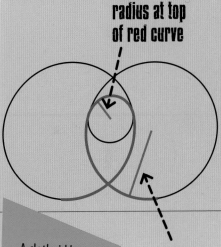

radius at top of red curve

radius at bottom of red curve

A clothoid loop has a smaller radius at the top, forming a tighter curve. This makes the car accelerate faster when it is upside down. The shallower curves at the sides slow the car slightly so it does not lose control going in or out of the loop-the-loop.

ACTIVITY: Loop-the-Bucket

Roller coaster designers say that people would not fall out of roller coaster cars upside down at the top of a loop-the-loop if they had no safety bars, due to the forces holding them in their seats. It's not a good idea to test this, but you can carry out a simple experiment to demonstrate the forces in action.

1 Tie the string with a secure knot to the center of the bucket handle. Adjust the string length so that you can hold one end with the bucket around 4 in. (10 cm) above the ground.

2 Put one penny in the bucket. Stand in enough space so you can swing the bucket safely. Swing the bucket forward, then backward with bigger and bigger swings. When the bucket is swinging high, start to rotate the bucket vertically in one direction in complete loop-the-loops.

!

SAFETY! Make sure there is no one else around when you start swinging the bucket!

24

3 Observe what happens to the penny. What happens when you swing the bucket more slowly? Finish the demonstration with gradually smaller swings before bringing the bucket to rest.

4 Now, repeat steps 2 and 3 using 20 pennies in the bucket. What was different this time?

Conclusion

The bucket travels in a circle because of centripetal force through the string toward your hand and shoulder. Objects stay inside the bucket because of the pull from its base toward them, opposing centripetal force. Pennies stay inside even when the bucket is upside down because the centripetal force is greater than the pull of gravity on its contents. You should find that you need to pull harder on the string and spin the bucket faster to make more pennies, with a greater total mass, stay inside the bucket. When the speed of rotation is too low, the string goes slack and the bucket cannot complete loops. Then the coins could tumble out.

What Roller Coaster Features Are There?

Without features like hills and loop-the-loops, a trip on a roller coaster would be no more exciting than a train ride. Roller coaster designers have invented all sorts of features to surprise and excite riders on their visits to the amusement park.

What is a corkscrew?

A corkscrew is a series of twisty downhill turns. Looking down the track, they look like lots of concentric circles, and from the side like a spring that has been stretched out. In a sequence, they make riders confused about which way up they are and let them experience lots of g-forces. Unlike loop-the-loops, riding a corkscrew maintains kinetic energy for the rest of the ride.

You can see three coils of the large corkscrew in this roller coaster ride. Just imagine how it would feel flying through them!

1 2 3

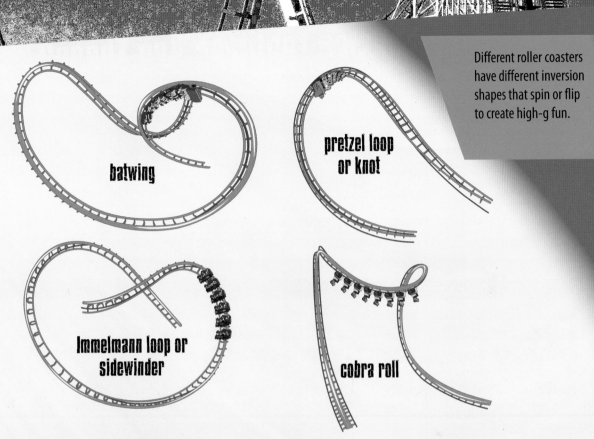

Different roller coasters have different inversion shapes that spin or flip to create high-g fun.

batwing

pretzel loop or knot

Immelmann loop or sidewinder

cobra roll

Upside-down features

Sea serpent, pretzel roll, inverted top hat, flying snake dive, and batwing: designers have created lots of loops, dives, twists, and roll features with unusual names that are often based on their shapes. These features are called **inversions** because they are included on rides to flip riders upside down. One of the most famous inversions is called the Immelmann loop, which is named after a World War I fighter pilot's flying maneuver. Like many inversions, it works by making the track twist from the top of its supports to the underside. This makes the car roll over as it moves along.

Special effects

The thrill of the roller coaster also relies on special effects. Some roller coasters go inside buildings or tunnels where it is dark. Other roller coasters travel through water-filled splashdowns. Some cars have scoops that make water shoot upward in jets when they pass through the water. But one of the most dramatic special effects is much simpler. A headchopper is a piece of track or support that the roller coaster runs under. Most riders duck, but they easily fit through the gap under a headchopper without losing their heads!

How Do Bumper Cars Work?

Bumper cars are plastic cars with small wheels that are hidden by a thick rubber bumper all the way around. When you press the floor pedal or accelerator, the car moves across the racetrack using an electric motor. If bumper cars used electrical energy through cables to power their motors, the cables would get tangled up. Batteries would be heavy and keep running down. So, bumper cars get the energy from around them. In some bumper car rides, the pole on the car touches the metal mesh ceiling and brushes under the car to touch the floor. This completes an **electrical circuit** so that electricity can flow into the motor. In other bumper car rides, the circuit is completed through brushes on the car and metal bars built into the floor. The steering wheel can be turned all the way around to go forward, sideways, and in reverse.

Bumper car forces

Bumper cars at rest have balanced forces. Pressing the accelerator unbalances the forces, as motion in one direction is greater than the force of friction from the wheels on the track in the other direction. When another car crashes into it, the forces in both cars become unbalanced even more. They may move faster, slow down, or change direction after the impact.

GRAPHITE

Graphite is a material made from carbon. In graphite, the carbon particles are arranged in sheets that are weakly linked to each other. That means they can slide over each other easily. Pencil lead is made from graphite because the layers can easily rub off onto paper. Many bumper car tracks are sprinkled with graphite powder, since this helps reduce friction under the car wheels.

You can feel the force when bumper cars collide and bounce off each other!

bounce (reaction)

bounce (reaction)

rubber bumper

thrust (action)

thrust (action)

How does motion change after a bump?

When bumper cars collide, you can feel your head or your whole body snapping toward the other car. The jolt happens because, even though the car has stopped, the mass of your body is continuing in the previous direction of motion. This resistance to a change in direction is called **inertia**.

Inertia is greater in heavier objects, such as people. So, when a heavy rider in one car bumps a lighter rider's car, the lighter rider will jolt more. That person's car is also pushed away more than the heavy one, because it requires less force to do so. When cars are of equal weight, they will bounce off each other by an equal distance.

The jolt of a bumper car impact rarely hurts, and riders aren't thrown out of the car because they wear seat belts.

NEWTON'S LAWS AND BUMPER CARS

Isaac Newton was a scientist. In the 17th century, he wrote three laws that describe all motion in action, including those on a bumper car ride.

	What the law says	What it does on the bumper cars
FIRST LAW	Every moving or resting object continues moving or resting unless an outside force acts on it.	You feel a jolt when bumper cars collide.
SECOND LAW	The greater the mass of an object, the harder it is to change its speed.	Lighter people are jolted and moved more than heavier ones on bumper cars.
THIRD LAW	For every action, there is an equal and opposite reaction.	When one bumper car hits another, they both move in opposite directions.

Soak up the shock

The rubber bumpers around the cars are not there for decoration. Their job is to absorb some of the impact. Seat belts also prevent inertia from making occupants fly out or bang into things. The bumper also has another trick up its sleeve. It changes an intense short bump into a longer-lasting experience.

The jolt is gentler and there is less deceleration when bumper cars hit at an angle rather than head-on.

ACTIVITY: Floating Bumper Cars

Construct a very basic bumper car that uses a layer of air to push it up and reduce the force of friction underneath.

1 Push the CD on a smooth surface, such as a table, floor, or kitchen surface. How far did it go?

2 Ask for an adult's help and stick the sports bottle lid over the hole in the CD using the hot glue gun. The idea is to create an airtight seal between the CD and the bottle lid.

3 Push down the top of the bottle lid to close it. Now inflate the balloon, twist the end to stop air from escaping, and stretch it over the lid.

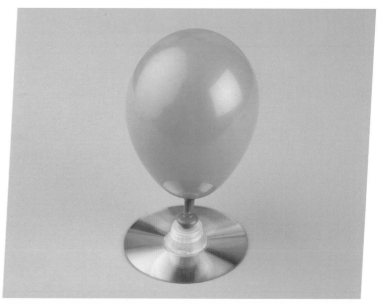

4 Place the modified CD on the smooth surface, pull up the lid to release air from the balloon, and push the CD with the same force as before. Did it move more smoothly and faster than the CD with no balloon?

5 Repeat the demonstration using the larger balloon, and then increase the car's mass using some modeling clay on top of the CD. How did its movement change?

Conclusion

The airflow from the balloon creates a cushion of moving air between the underside of the disc and the surface underneath. This lifts the CD and reduces contact between the materials. With less friction, the balloon bumper car can move faster and with less effort. As the balloon empties, it is less stretched and pushes less on the remaining air inside, so friction increases. With a larger balloon, the air cushion should last longer. With extra weight on the CD, the airflow from the balloon should be too weak to lift its greater mass.

How Does a Simulator Ride Work?

Riders on one of the most popular amusement park machines get their thrills without actually going anywhere. A **simulator** ride uses a combination of moving seats and on-screen action to trick the riders' senses into believing they are experiencing extreme forces.

Riders on a simulator sit in the dark apart from the on-screen action. The movements of the simulator trick them into thinking they are having a real ride.

Moving box

The simulators at most amusement parks are enclosed boxes, sometimes shaped like spacecraft. Inside, there are rows of seats for riders that face a screen. Underneath, there are several powerful **hydraulic jacks** supporting the simulator. Liquid is forced at high pressure inside these jacks to push the end up or down. By mounting the jacks at different points on the simulator, it can be tilted in any direction.

Ride in the dark

The movements of the simulator are coordinated with what happens during a video presentation on the screen. Riders sit in the dark and view a journey on a train, plane, spaceship, or other vehicle. It can be a film of a real ride, but it is often a realistic 3-D animation. Riders view the movement as if they are looking forward from the front of the vehicle. The jacks tip the simulator back and forth so riders feel the journey as changing forces from their seats.

PILOT TRAINERS

The first simulators were built for pilots to learn about flying without the expense and danger of actually being in the air. Early 20th-century simulators were model planes with **cockpits**, in which trainee pilots could operate levers to make the plane move up and down. By the 1980s, pilots could simulate flying in realistic cockpits, using controls that moved miniature cameras over highly detailed models of landscapes. Today's simulators are like sophisticated versions of amusement park rides, in which the trainees are controlling realistic action in 3-D on wrap-around screens and feeling forces from movements of the simulator.

What we see and hear on a ride helps us figure out our position, distance, and speed relative to the ground and surrounding objects.

Experiencing a ride

How we feel the rides at an amusement park depends on many senses working together. Much of this is visual. Light **receptors** in our eyes detect changing patterns of light and color that our brains use to interpret the world around us. Our ears also hear changing volumes of noises to figure out where we are.

Feeling the forces

We can also feel forces because of what goes on inside our **inner ears**. When our heads move, fluid shifts through narrow canals in our ears and bends tiny hairs that contain movement receptors. Even if our eyes are closed, our brains interpret these movements to detect rotation. Other pressure receptors around our bodies, such as those in skin, muscles, and joints, help us feel pushes and pulls caused by changes in motion.

Simulator trickery

A simulator tricks these senses. Inside, the only sights and sounds are from the screen, so riders get no clues about their real position from the real world. But making the images of the virtual on-screen surroundings fly past, and tilting the seats backward to increase the push on their backs, makes riders feel they are accelerating forward. Simulators can also fool you into thinking you are turning sharply, diving, and decelerating. However, they cannot fool riders' inner ears that they are rotating, no matter how realistic the movement appears on-screen!

Some people feel sick on amusement park rides such as the pendulum because their senses are confused!

MOTION SICKNESS

On a pendulum ride, you see a regular motion and remain the same distance from other riders. Yet your inner ears and pressure receptors, including those in the stomach, detect acceleration and frequent changes in g-forces. So, your brain gets confused and it sends stress chemicals to the stomach. That's why you might feel motion sickness!

Can I Have Thrills without Spills?

The fear you feel on the most extreme rides is your body's natural response to its sense of danger. But don't worry. Amusement parks focus on safety as well as fun.

Park workers regularly inspect the condition of tracks and maintain the wheels, brakes, motors, and other moving parts on rides.

Before being used in ride construction, materials are carefully tested for their strength and durability.

Safety in numbers

Amusement parks are very popular. In the United States alone, around a third of a billion people visit amusement parks each year. Of these, only around 1,400 need medical assistance as a result of going to the park. That's a tiny fraction of 1 percent of visitors. Most of these have minor bumps caused by not following safety rules. It is not the extreme rides that cause the most injuries. One of the most common injuries is a bump on the head after falling from a horse on the carousel!

Safe design and operation

All rides are designed and constructed with safety in mind. Brakes exert more friction than is actually needed to stop a moving roller coaster car. Hills and curves are sized and shaped so they do not create unsafe amounts of centripetal and g-forces. Computer systems are used to control the speed of cars, the distance between them, and any obstructions on tracks.

HIGH-G EFFECTS

The fastest amusement park rides, such as loop-the-loops, take riders up to about 3 or 4 g. Pilots blasting upward in space rockets or fighter jets turning at high speed may experience up to 12 g. At this acceleration, their blood would flow toward their feet due to inertia, which might cause them to faint because their brain does not have enough blood. So, pilots wear special suits that press on their blood vessels, to stop the blood from moving to the wrong places.

Did You Feel the Force?

Most people's memories of a day at the amusement park include the bright lights and colors, the looks on excited, happy, and scared faces, and the sounds of joy and terror. But the real stars of the show are silent, invisible, powerful forces that make the rides such an assault on our senses.

Stars of the show

The main acts are gravity, acceleration, friction, and centripetal forces. But they rely on a supporting cast. These include other invisible assistants, such as inertia and potential and kinetic energy. They also include the rides themselves, from the shapes of the curves and loops, to the devices that send roller coasters to the top of their first hill and those that stop machines from speeding out of control. The whole production is the work of park designers, safety experts, and, of course, the riders themselves!

Freefall Xtreme and other wind tunnel rides are massive, upward-pointing fans. Riders can float on the spot, cheating gravity.

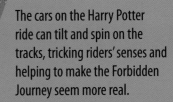

Old and new

Some park rides have been with us for years, such as the merry-go-round and rotor. But designers have had to build bigger, faster, and more exciting rides over time to keep the crowds visiting amusement parks. In the mid-1960s, the highest roller coaster was 100 feet (30 meters), but today, some tower nearly five times that height and reach speeds of 150 miles (240 kilometers) per hour.

Today, many people are used to playing exciting video games with virtual thrills and spills in their homes, so amusement park designers are constantly developing new rides to attract the crowds. For example, the riders on "Harry Potter and the Forbidden Journey" sit on benches moved around by robotic arms mounted on tracks, which move past 3-D screens and through spaces based on the Harry Potter movie sets. It is a cross between a simulator and a real ride with some real forces. Just imagine what rides will be like in the future!

1 The initial potential energy of a roller coaster is changed into what after it crests the first hill?
    a) more potential energy
    b) electrical energy
    c) light energy
    d) kinetic energy

2 What are the two main forces acting on a roller coaster car going downhill?
    a) gravity and acceleration
    b) gravity and friction
    c) acceleration and deceleration
    d) friction and acceleration

3 Newton's first law of motion says that an object in motion tends to do what?
    a) pick up friction
    b) stay in motion
    c) eventually stop moving
    d) accelerate

4 When an object falls, air resistance:
    a) acts in the opposite direction than the weight
    b) acts in the same direction as the weight
    c) acts at right angles to the weight
    d) does not act at all

5 If gravity pulls you toward the center of Earth, why don't you fall through the floor?
    a) because gravity runs out
    b) because gravity doesn't act through hard floors
    c) because the floor exerts an equal force to gravity in the opposite direction
    d) because of friction

6 What force pulling an object moving in a circle prevents it from flying off in a straight line?
a) centrifugal force
b) inertia
c) centripetal force
d) friction

7 Which two of the following are not forces?
a) mass
b) gravity
c) height
d) thrust

8 When an object is at rest or stationary:
a) there are no forces acting on it
b) there are forces acting on it, but they are balanced
c) there is just one force, gravity, acting on it
d) there are forces acting on it, but they are unbalanced

9 Which of the following is a change of motion?
a) speed
b) inertia
c) acceleration
d) friction

10 When you are falling on a drop tower and experiencing weightlessness, the g-force you feel is:
a) exactly 1 g
b) 2 g
c) 10 g
d) zero g

Glossary

accelerate move more quickly; speed up

air resistance force that slows down the movement of an object through the air

balanced when two forces acting on an object are equal in size but act in opposite directions, we say that they are balanced forces

centripetal force force that makes an object follow a curved path that is pointed toward the center point the object moves around. Spin a toy on a string and the centripetal force is toward your hand.

cockpit compartment where pilot and other crew members of an aircraft sit and work

deceleration slowing down or negative acceleration

electrical circuit unbroken path along which electrical energy or electricity flows to make electrical devices work

force a push or a pull on an object. A force gives energy to an object.

friction force produced when one surface moves over another surface. Friction acts to slow down the movement.

g-force measure of how much force acts on a person or an object compared with the normal weight force due to Earth's gravity

gravity force of attraction between two objects. On Earth, gravity pulls everything toward the ground. This is because Earth's mass is much greater than everything around it.

hydraulic jack machine that uses trapped liquid in tubes to create pushes and pulls

inertia resistance to change in direction or speed. Inertia is greater in objects with greater mass.

inner ear part of the ear inside our head. It detects sounds and gravity, which helps us keep our balance.

inversion stretches of roller coaster rides when people are suspended upside down

kinetic energy energy a moving object has because it is moving

mass amount of matter or physical substance something has. Weight is related to mass because weight measures the force of gravity on the mass of an object.

noncontact force force that acts on an object without touching it, such as magnetism or gravity

potential energy ability to do work caused by an object's position, tension, electric charge, or other factors. For example, a crushed spring and a book high on a shelf both have potential energy.

receptor special cell in living things that can detect changes in light, pressure, and other stimuli

revolution complete turn or spin around a fixed point. Spinning speed is often expressed in revolutions per minute, or rpm.

simulator machine in some amusement parks that mimics a real ride using film and the movements of people's seats

terminal velocity constant speed that a falling object reaches when air resistance balances gravity

unbalanced when one force acting on an object is greater in size than the other force, we say that they are unbalanced forces

vertical upright or at right angles to the horizontal

weightlessness floating feeling people get when there is no force of support on their body

zero g when there is no apparent force of gravity acting on a body

Books

Brush, Jim. *Roller Coasters* (Fast Facts). Mankato, Minn.: Sea-to-Sea, 2012.

Claybourne, Anna. *Gut-Wrenching Gravity and Other Fatal Forces* (Disgusting and Dreadful Science). St. Catharines, Ont.: Crabtree, 2013.

Dicker, Katie. *Forces and Motion* (Sherlock Bones Looks at Physical Science). New York: Windmill, 2011.

Royston, Angela. *Forces and Motion* (Essential Physical Science). Chicago: Heinemann Library, 2014.

Web sites

FactHound offers a safe, fun way to find Internet sites related to this book. All of the sites on FactHound have been researched by our staff.

Here's all you do:

Visit www.facthound.com

Type in this code: 9781484625989

Places to visit

The Exploratorium
Pier 15
(Embarcadero at Green Street)
San Francisco, California 94111
www.exploratorium.edu

This is a great museum that lets kids explore science with lots of amazing hands-on exhibits.

There are thousands of amusement parks worldwide, including these thrilling ones in the United States:

- Busch Gardens, Williamsburg, Virginia — **seaworldparks.com/en/ buschgardens-williamsburg/**

- Cedar Point, Sandusky, Ohio — **www.cedarpoint.com**
- Six Flags Great America, Gurnee, Illinois — **www.sixflags.com/greatamerica**

Further research

- Research amusement parks worldwide and then create a global map of attractions. Where are the highest and fastest rides or the tallest drop towers? From your research, do you think that amusement parks are distributed evenly around the globe, or only in particular continents or countries? Do they correspond with the population and average income (GDP) of each country? Why do you think this is?

- Build your own roller coaster using foam pipe insulation tube for a track and marbles for cars (see www.msichicago.org/online-science/activities/activity-detail/activities/build-a-roller-coaster/). Experiment with different shaped loop-the-loops, twists, and other features. Can you make your marble experience an inversion?

- Amusement parks are at particular fixed places, but many people can also experience rides at traveling carnivals and fairs. Research the history of carnivals and fairs. Have they always been just for amusement?

Index